LOOK BACK OSSETT

NORMAN ELLIS

2007

First published in 2007 by
Rickaro Books, Horbury.

© Norman Ellis

ISBN: 978 09546439 2 8
Limited to 500 copies

Rickaro Books, 17 High Street,
Horbury, Wakefield WF4 5AB

Printed by N.M. Print Services
Telephone: 01924 382552

Front cover
On a showery day in 1967, the Gawthorpe Maypole procession passes in front of Ossett Town Hall, and features the Woodhead float carrying a simulated version of one of the famous shock absorbers.

Preface

On Sunday morning 12 July 1987, I heard a knock on my door. I opened it to find Mike Coupland, chief draughtsman at Woodhead Manufacturing Company, where I worked, standing there. This, I thought, could only mean I had been sacked or made redundant. A concerned Michael quickly informed me that there had been a fire at the Woodhead offices. These were located on the upper floor of the old Northfield Mill on Church Street. The damage was, it seemed, extensive. I said I would go down and have a look (I lived a ten minute walk away). Perhaps callously, I took my camera. Externally, there was little sign of damage. At first my request to go inside was refused; then I was told I could enter if I donned a hard hat. Wearing one of these, I climbed the stone steps to the upper floor.

The extent of the disaster soon became shockingly apparent. The fire damage had been compounded by water damage, the suspended ceiling having crashed down and turned to soggy pulp. The drawing office, its adjacent file and print room, the telex office and the sales and accounts departments were worst affected. The purchase and wages sections, plus the typing area, were less damaged. The offices on the ground floor had suffered, mainly because of water seepage.

By Monday morning, the full magnitude of the damage became more obvious. Much of the firm's paperwork was severely damaged or lost. Within a few days, 63,000 drawings, some of them going back forty years, were shipped away for drying, cleaning and microfilming. Led by managing director, Mr G R Harrison, workpeople buckled in and rescued as much as possible of the damaged furniture and carpeting. Staff were rehoused in any available space. I and a number of my colleagues ended up in the old canteen at the Kingsway end.

The 63,000 microfilms were eventually delivered. These had been placed in card mounts, similar to slide mounts, and could be copied on a special machine. Having worked at Woodhead since 1950, I inherited the task of sorting and indexing the microfilms. I completed this task just before taking voluntary redundancy in late 1988.

I recalled the time back in 1950 when I had an almost grandstand view of a fire at the Pickles, Ayland Company's Sowdill Works. These were situated on the site of today's Wilman post and Laurel Crescent. Pickles, Ayland were painting contractors (they once painted York Station). They also manufactured paint and varnish. I was then new to Woodhead Monroe (later Woodhead Manufacturing) and worked in a small drawing office up some steps at the Kingsway end. Suddenly one morning, Bill Duckett, the chief draughtsman, saw smoke surging to the sky where Sowdill Works were located. Bill, draughtsman Jim Kershaw and I watched the billowing black smoke from our vantage point.

I got my photographs of the Woodhead fire damage, but have none of the Pickles, Ayland catastrophe. Over the years, I snapped the various floats which the Woodhead people decorated for the Gawthorpe Maypole and other events. Photography had been my hobby since the 1950s. Collecting old postcards, photographs and ephemera came a little later. One day, a Woodhead employee was clearing out a drawer and found a small file of Woodhead photographs. They were destined for the waste-paper basket, but I managed to rescue them. This book is a compilation of some of the above items – and much more. Call me a hoarder if you like!

This is the second book I have written on Ossett; the first, titled *Bygone Ossett,* sold extremely well. Only a few copies of it remain for sale. Interestingly, Stan Barstow, the author of *A Kind of Loving* and other books, worked for a short time on the next drawing board to me at Woodhead Monroe.

Acknowledgements and Sources

Gwyneth H Stansfield, *A Threefold Cord,* c.1975.
Alan Allsopp, *Better by Far,* Miniprint Dewsbury, 1979.
John Pollard, *Glimpses of Ossett's History,* Ossett & District Historical Society, 1983.
Cockburn's Ossett, Ossett & District Historical Society, 1987.
John Goodchild, *Ossett on Old Picture Postcards,* European Library, 1993.
Norman Ellis, *Bygone Ossett,* Rickaro Books, 2003.
Newspapers: *Dewsbury Reporter* and *Ossett Observer,* various issues.
Kelly's Directories, Ordnance Survey Maps, Guide Books.
Postcards and photographs are credited individually if their origination is known.

I was always grateful for the help and encouragement I received from Jean Crabtree (nee Fisher) who sadly died in January 2007. Jean was well immersed in the history of Ossett. She was employed for a time at Woodheads. Her mother, Mary Fisher, also worked there, supplying tea and snacks from a trolley to the office staff. She passed away in October 1997, aged 92 years. Jean's lovely daughter, Julie, also joined the Woodhead clan for a time.

Introduction

Ossett's only post office used to be situated at the lower end of Dale Street. The postman was known as Tommy Post. Letters were brought by road and horse from Wakefield and delivered by Tommy and his son, who at the same time collected others for the next despatch. Receiving a letter was a rarity, except for those engaged in business. The only newspaper circulating in the area was the *Leeds Mercury,* costing 4 ½ d. This was an expensive luxury, so several people clubbed together to buy a copy. It was read aloud and then passed around for private perusal. The *Ossett Observer* was launched in 1864.

In 1894, the Post Office gave private publishers license to produce postcards. Within a few years, some of the postcards had acquired a small pictorial content. This was gradually increased in area, although the message still had to be written on the same side as the picture. By the early 1900s, postcards were being posted privately between friends, either from people on holiday or to arrange a meeting. By 1904, the pictorial aspect of the card was as important as the message and usually covered most of one side.

Topographical picture postcards, for example those showing a church, street or event, are now a valuable source for social historians. Those with an image produced from a glass plate in a small back-street studio are often unique. The first Ossett picture postcards seem to date from 1904. By then, the *Ossett Observer* had also become a mine of local information, whether it was a report of a fire at a local mill, a Whit walk or seven days for being drunk and disorderly. This book relies heavily on the local 'rag' and the picture postcard.

Back in the 1860s, the nucleus of Ossett consisted of one main thoroughfare – Dale Street leading through the town to the Market Place, Bank Street, Queen Street and The Green. The Market Place contained the old Chapel-of-Ease and the Grammar School. Near the chapel was a stable for the use of worshippers riding there on horseback. Surrounding the area were buildings of mixed appearance, some of whose occupants kept pigs.

Church Street, then called Dark Lane or Field Lane, was a private road with a chain across to prevent unlawful use. Wesley Street, called Pildacre Lane, was a narrow lane with a dyke at one side, down which the sewage ran. This was a characteristic of other parts of the town. When the roads became impassable due to horses and carts, a few loads of dross were thrown on to them. For the public water supply, communal wells were constructed, although the affluent residents had their own supply. Illness was rife; the fear of an epidemic was ever present.

The Hare & Hounds on Queen Street was the meeting place of sporting men, where *Bell's Life,* a publication devoted to accounts of prize-fighting, was read aloud. Prize fights, cock fights and bull fights in Ossett itself had virtually become diversions of the past. In the many Ossett pubs, there were no strictly applied licensing laws for the sale of alcoholic beverages. But on the Sabbath day, closing was compulsory during the hours of public worship. The period from 1857 to 1867 witnessed an abundance of chapel and church building in Ossett, although it was some time before the various denominations developed a full social conscience in addition to a spiritual one.

Around the year 1900, there were two dozen places of worship in the Borough of Ossett, including three parish churches – one each for the parishes of Ossett, South Ossett and Gawthorpe. The balance mostly consisted of Nonconformist denominations. Three distinct branches of Methodism were represented – Wesleyans, Primitives and United Methodists. Complementary to these were the Congregationalists and the Baptists. The branches of Nonconformity tended to mix like oil and water, at least up to the 1950s, although some of the competition between the chapels was probably healthy. By the early 1900s, they were meeting an important social need, with their football, cricket and tennis clubs, plus other convivial activities. The pews were well-filled on a Sunday, and the Sunday schools were well-attended. Churches and chapels, with all their faults and foibles, were a way of life for many, but all this was set to change eventually.

Education in Ossett was a hit and miss affair, at least up to the early 1900s. The Grammar School in the Market Place had developed from a school founded by the SPCK in the 1730s to teach the three Rs. Gawthorpe had a school by 1750, erected by public subscription. There were a few small private schools. In 1870, the Forster Education Act was passed to encourage the formation of local board schools, although it was several years before any such schools were opened in Ossett, the first being in the Baptist schoolroom at Spa Street and the Bethel Congregational Chapel at Flushdyke. The Balfour Education Act of 1902, which made local councils responsible for education, was not adopted by the Borough of Ossett until 1904. Spa Street and Flushdyke became council schools in 1906.

The Grammar School began a fresh era at South Ossett in 1906. The new Southdale Council School was opened in 1908. Bethel Chapel became too small, so the new Flushdyke Council School was built, which opened in 1912. The new Gawthorpe Council School opened its doors in 1927. The Mechanics' Institute on Station Road also served as a Technical School.

The motto incorporated on Ossett's coat of arms translates to *"Useless things made useful by skill"*. This is an apt reference to the conversion of rags and woollen waste into mungo and shoddy to produce profitable goods. The town's establishment as a woollen centre can be traced back to its cottage industry. By the early 1700s, handloom weavers were working long hours at home to produce broadcloth. Several families branched out and built small mills, perhaps employing only twenty people. Even the larger mills were small compared with those of other towns.

In 1813, at nearby Batley, the processing of woollen rags was developed. Waste woollen material was broken down to a fibrous state and worked with virgin wool to make mungo and shoddy. Ossett became an important centre for these products; its 'rag trade' was born. Rags were delivered to the town from a wide area and sorted according to colour and quality, sometimes by women working at home. After being torn to pieces on a grinder, the fibres were drawn off the machine and mixed with new wool ready for spinning. Mungo was produced from the short soft wools, whilst shoddy came from the longer and firmer wools. Around 1910, there were ninety rag merchants and eighteen manufacturers of mungo and shoddy in the borough.

Another of Ossett's important industries was coal mining. Low Laithes Colliery closed down in 1926. The last pits to shut were Old Roundwood in 1966 and Shaw Cross in 1968. The latter was just over the border with Dewsbury but employed many Ossett men. Other industries had sprung up, including those that were connected with mining or textiles. A surprising newcomer in 1948 was the Leeds firm of Jonas Woodhead, who proceeded to make coil springs and shock absorbers in premises between Church Street and Kingsway. Woodhead became Ossett's biggest employer.

The man who gave his name to Richard Sutcliffe Limited was a mining engineer and a pioneer of underground conveyors and coal cutting machines. His first factory was established at Horbury in 1905. To increase output, a second factory was set up at Healey Road, Ossett, in 1947. An associated company, Sutcliffe Moulded Rubber, was founded in 1947. Its Impact Works was located on Church Street. Spencer & Halstead was incorporated in 1912, occupying a corrugated iron workshop on Northfield Road, with twelve employees. When expansion was no longer practical, the firm moved to much larger premises in Wakefield Road, Flushdyke. Their specialities included fans, blast cleaning plant and dust and fume extraction systems.

A handbook published in 1959 by Ossett Corporation laid great emphasis on the local industries. It sang the praises of a canned foods importer, S D Mathews Ltd. In November 1955, seven men had met in an empty office in Park Square and, assisted by a few cases of ale, baptised Ossett as their new headquarters. They were soon able to boast about their imports of hams from Germany, ox tongues from Australia, refined lard from Chicago. Some firms became household names in the town, for example Burdekin's for baskets, Mickman's for hosiery or George Bennett for coal and coke. Less well-known was the firm of Joseph Redgewick & Sons, which made rag grinding machines. The handbook listed fifteen firms (and there were others) which were still involved in the various processes of producing mungo and shoddy. This included Harold Bagley of Church Street, Bickle Brothers of Northfield Mill, J E Glover of Wesley Street and Greenfield Mills, E N Harrop of Royds Mills and Jessop Brothers of Springfield Mills.

Much of the centre of Ossett which is visible today is a product of the latter part of the nineteenth century and the first decade of the twentieth century. An 1875 Local Act of Parliament gave Ossett borrowing powers to spend up to £50,000 on street improvements, water supply and sewage disposal. The Wakefield & Barnsley Union Bank was opened in 1870; the London City & Midland Bank in 1892. The first sod for Station Road was cut in 1888. This thoroughfare soon acquired numerous fine buildings, including the Mechanics' Institute (1889), Liberal Club (1893) and Yorkshire Penny Bank (1893), although this started life as a post office and chemist's shop. The Town Hall was opened in 1908.

The Market Place underwent a series of changes – areas of grass, raised flower beds, trees and shrubs. It was asserted that people were afraid to pass through after dark. Overall, the latest layout, with block paving, bears striking resemblance to that of 1908. On two days a week, and sometimes three, the Market Place lives up to its name and hosts a market, with a good cross-section of traders. Standing beside the Market Place is the shop of Ossett Newsagents, from which premises it is believed the *Ossett Observer* has been sold for the longest period. In the early 1900s, the shop belonged to Nettleton & Mitchell, who were newsagents there for about fifty years. Then came F & J R Shaw, followed by Mr Perkin and Mr Turner.

In 1974, the Borough of Ossett lost some of its autonomy when it became part of the Wakefield Metropolitan District. What is its future? By 2058, will the Town Hall have been replaced by a multi-storey car park? Will Green Park have become a helicopter pad? Will every household have eight wheelie bins? Will the water tower at Gawthorpe have been replaced with a huge viewing wheel? And will Ossett's last fish-and-chip shop (and the last in Yorkshire) have become a 'chippie' museum?

In 1927, the Borough of Ossett was offering for sale, at cost price, houses at £450 each. *"The houses are situate at Leeds Road (one minute from trams and buses) and are most desirable and convenient residences"*. Perhaps Ossett was then a good place to live. Mungo and shoddy are now largely the stuff of history. The replacement industries have tended to become concentrated on the Sandbeds and Longlands areas of the town, with a plethora of relatively small units. The mill town has become a commuter town, with residential developments springing up everywhere. Because of mineral springs, there were plans right up to the 1880s to turn parts of Ossett into another Harrogate. The project was abandoned, although Spa Street and Spa Lane remain. Ossett will not become another spa town, but the retention of our green areas must be an important part of any future developments.

1. Aerial view shows Ossett in 1939. *Photograph.*

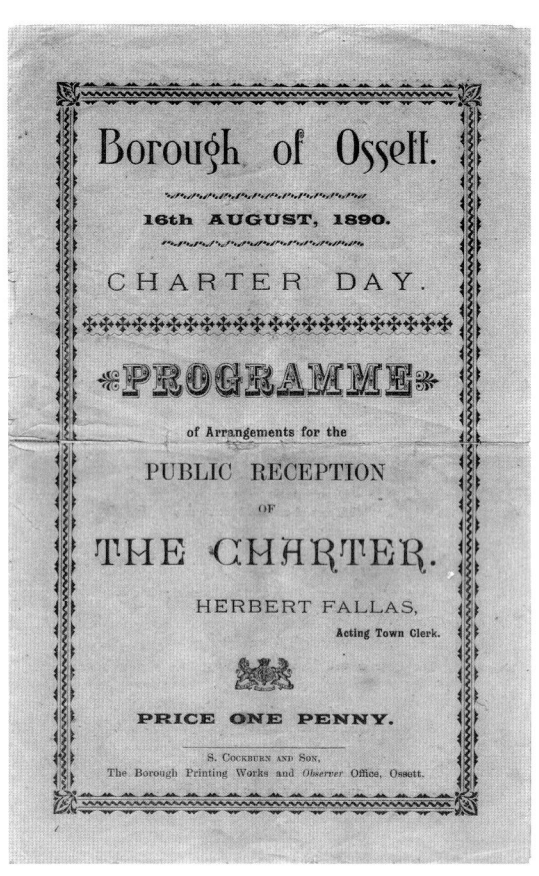

2. Dewsbury's plans to extend its borough boundaries into Ossett prompted Ossett to apply for a Charter of Incorporation as a borough. This was granted on 30 June 1890. On the morning of 16 August 1890, the charter arrived at Ossett Station and was carried into town in a procession, which included Ossett Brass & Reed Band, mounted police, members of Ossett Local Board and various public bodies. The Charter was read in the Market Place and the Gawthorpe Victoria Band played. A public luncheon was provided in a large marquee on the football field near the railway station. In the afternoon, a larger procession assembled in the Market Place. It included children from the various church and nonconformist schools. The route was along Dale Street, Church Street, Wakefield Road, Dale Street, Bank Street, The Green, Manor Road, Station Road, and back to the Market Place. This procession, with the Charter, was led by the Band of the King's Own Yorkshire Light Infantry and other bands. It included several carriages holding civic dignitaries and others. Free tea was provided for children at various locations. The evening entertainment, in the field near the station, included a military tournament, minstrels and Punch & Judy. The whole was rounded off with a fireworks display by Riley's of Ossett.

Supplement to the "OSSETT OBSERVER" of Saturday, August 23rd, 1890.

4. This and the next three photographs show Ossett Market Place in 1904. The old Trinity Church which stood there was demolished in 1866, leaving the Old Grammar School on the right as the centre's main building. To its left is Dale Street and at extreme left is a grocer's, newsagent's and tobacconist's shop, currently known as Ossett Newsagents. *Postcard.*

5. The Pickard Memorial Fountain on the right, with troughs for horses and dogs, was provided in 1893 by Hannah Pickard, a member of an Ossett textile family. Behind it is the beginning of Town End. In the centre are the premises of John William Cudworth, painter and decorator, who later moved to Dale Street. *Postcard.*

6. The London City & Midland Bank of 1892 dominates this view, with the boot, shoe and legging shop of Salter & Salter on the left. Shawled women and carts delivering coal were familiar sights at this period. *Postcard.*

7. The Market Place, much of it laid with granite setts, underwent some upheaval in 1904 when tram lines were laid. Looking down Bank Street from the Market Place, this is the first day of public tramway operation on 15 August 1904. The yard of the Cock & Bottle is to the left of the nearest tram. *Postcard.*

8. Following discussions stretching back to 1856, the foundation stone for Ossett Town Hall was laid on Shrove Tuesday 27 February 1906 by the Mayor, Councillor J Hampshire Nettleton. It was officially opened on Tuesday 2 June 1908. A proportion of the estimated 12,000 people who gathered for the ceremony is pictured from the Town Hall, with the end of Station Road at the back. Roof tops and the fountain are in use as vantage points. *Postcard.*

9. The Mayor, Councillor J T Marsden, on a raised platform in front of the Town Hall, speaks at the opening ceremony on 2 June, before declaring the building open. The celebrations continued into the evening, some of them being held in Gedham Field, where Punch & Judy proved popular. The festivities lasted until Thursday when the old folks were entertained. *Postcard: Leeds Mercury.*

10. The Barnsley firm of Warner Gothard specialised in producing postcards of special events. Their Dewsbury branch produced this montage. It commemorates the opening of Ossett Town Hall and includes the Mayor and his spouse. *Postcard: A F Gothard, Dewsbury.*

11. The Town Hall is shown festooned for its opening day ceremony. The beautifully finished stone work includes the Ossett coat-of-arms at roof level above the main entrance. *Postcard.*

12. Ossett Town Hall in 1909. Apart from the addition of ramps to facilitate entry, the exterior of the building is little changed today. The same cannot be said of the fountain which, after years of neglect, was banished to Green Park. *Postcard.*

13. The public hall of the Town Hall, Ossett, shortly after opening day. It was designed to hold 1,300 people. *Postcard.*

14. The court room of the Town Hall soon after opening day. Previously, the premises housing the Mechanics' Institute and Municipal Technical School were used for court proceedings. On Monday 20 August !906, a hurrier, Blythe Walker, and a schoolboy, Herbert Richardson, were summoned before the court at the Municipal Technical School for playing cricket in the street at South Ossett. Following complaints, they were apprehended by Police Sergeant Henthorne, who confiscated their (tennis) ball. Each defendant pleaded guilty in court and was fined 1/- plus costs. *Postcard.*

15. Ossett Market Place became a focal point for many events. Here, the Town Hall has been decorated for the Coronation Festival on 22 June 1911. The photographer seems to have captured an almost entirely male group of participants – most of them wearing flat caps. *Postcard.*

16. This is the crowd which gathered in the Market Place for the Coronation Festival. The dais in front of the Town Hall is partly visible on the right, with, below it, a group of Boy Scouts. There were stipulations on where everyone was expected to stand for the formalities. What is now Richmond's shop is in the background. Further back, the large building is the Wesleyan Chapel. *Postcard: J Senior, photographer, Ossett.*

17. Their Majesties, King George V and Queen Mary, visited Ossett on Thursday 10 July 1912, as part of their itinerary through industrial towns of the West Riding. Here, in front of the Town Hall, top-hatted dignitaries ponder over the final arrangements, their wives seemingly having secured good seats. The decorations appear to be fine, but the carpet looks slightly tatty. *Postcard.*

18. On 10 July 1912, the King is welcomed to Ossett by the Mayor, Councillor H Robinson, and others. The Queen is probably concealed by the lady with the large hat. The London City & Midland Bank is in the background. *Postcard.*

19. After the 1914-18 War, Peace Celebrations were held in Ossett from 19 to 22 July 1919. Above, on the first day, the proclamation is being read in front of the Town Hall. Some of the buildings in the background (including B Dunford, tailor) were eventually demolished to accommodate Kingsway. *Postcard.*

20. On 6 May 1935, local celebrations for the Silver Jubilee of King George V and Queen Mary included another Market Place gathering and a service at the Parish Church. The Mayor of Ossett (from 1933 to 1937), Alderman Gladstone Moorhouse, is seen taking part in the event in front of the Town Hall. Note the microphone. Mr Moorhouse, who resided at Ivy Bank on Ryecroft Street, became a well-known local builder. He was a sidesman at the Parish Church. *Postcard.*

21. Market Place and Town Hall, c.1955. Incongruous concrete lamp standards have been erected. The entrance to the underground toilets is still visible beside a pair of telephone booths which hide the fountain. Within a few years, these gave way to a large grassed area. *Postcard: Lilywhite, Brighouse.*

22. The Town Hall in 1958. Telephone boxes have appeared beneath its shadow. A beat bobby, today a rare sight, looks nonchalantly across towards Kingsway. *Photograph: Joyce Petty, Ossett.*

23. Ossett Market Place from the Town Hall, looking along Bank Street in the early 1950s. The remains of the Pickard Memorial Fountain are sandwiched between the toilets and telephone booths, these items of street furniture having become a turning point for red Wakefield buses. The Hagenbach confectionery shop is on the left, at the corner with Station Road. Today, all this area is pedestrianised. *Postcard: W Fowler, photographer, Dale Street, Ossett.*

24. Ossett Market Place in late 2000, when new paving was being laid. At the time, Nettletons, bakers and formerly also butchers, were still trading from the attractive building on the left. They vacated the shop in 2001. *Photograph: N Ellis.*

25. Bank Street is pictured on a damp day in the winter of 1907-08. The Market Place and Town Hall are visible in the distance, the latter still requiring its clock tower. On the left, the shop of Hemingway Brothers has a good display. The imposing building further along is the Wakefield & Barnsley Union Bank. The single-storey timber building is the tripe shop of Herbert Oakes (nicknamed 'Holly Oaks'). It later became George Egan's cobblery shop. *Postcard.*

26. Dale Street, with some of the old Ossett Industrial Co-operative Society buildings on the left and the Horse & Jockey Inn on the right. The tramcar, having travelled from Dewsbury, is on the last lap of its journey to Ossett. *Postcard.*

27. The children's recreation ground on Church Street in the late 1950s. It is shown backed by Northfield Road and the Parish Church. *Postcard: Donald Peace, newsagent, 28 Dale Street, Ossett.*

28. Station Road, pictured here, was completed in 1889. It linked the Market Place with Park Square and served Ossett Station. It later formed part of the route for trams to Horbury, Wakefield and Agbrigg. West Riding tramcar number 22 is seen approaching the centre of Ossett in August 1904, its destination indicator already having been set for the return journey. *Postcard.*

29. The Public Library on Station Road. The council took over the Mechanics' Institute in 1898 for use as the library. Extensive refurbishment was carried out in 1935, the reopening ceremony being performed on 24 October by the Mayor, Councillor Gladstone Moorhouse. Eight days later, the new Ossett Corporation gas showroom, shown on the right, was opened in the same block by the Mayoress, Mrs Gladstone Moorhouse. *Postcard.*

30. Station Road before pedestrianisation. The Yorkshire Penny Bank building on the left originated as a post office and chemist's shop for J W Cussons, who became a soap manufacturer. The Liberal Club at extreme right was opened in 1893 for a society formed in 1874. Beyond it is the Library. *Postcard: F Frith & Co, Reigate.*

31. Station Road, c.1910, with the intersection of Prospect Road in the middle distance. The distant cart appears to be using the tram tracks! *Postcard.*

32. Further down Station Road, new building work consisted mainly of dwellings, as pictured here looking towards Park Square from the railway bridge. Observe the single set of tram lines and row of tram standards. *Postcard.*

33. Station Road, c.1905. The block of fine residences on the right, appropriately named The Gables, was constructed in 1897. The houses are also visible on the left of the previous picture. *Postcard.*

34. This part of Park Square (the west side) eventually formed part of Station Road, depicted here c.1912. The shop of Ezra Coldwell, grocer and provision dealer, is on the left, displaying enamel signs for Reckitt's Blue and Rowntree's Cocoa. Park Square, earlier known as Middle Common, became a small self-sufficient part of Ossett, much of its development occurring after 1850, when other nearby areas such as Ossett Green, Giggal Hill and Low Common had already witnessed much growth. By 1912, Park Square had a tailor, a carpenter, a painter, a coal agent, a tea agent and a beer retailer. There were two rag merchants, also manufacturers of mungo and sports goods. There was even a Unitarian Chapel, although many people probably trudged to Christ Church, South Ossett, consecrated in 1851. *Postcard: James Edward Shaw, wholesale stationer, 28 Bank Street, Ossett.*

35. Horbury Road, looking towards The Green, c.1912, with South Ossett Parish Church on the right. This road formed part of the direct highway from Ossett to Horbury before Station Road was constructed. *Postcard.*

36. West Wells, Ossett, with 'Sparrow Park' in the centre, c.1935. The large houses are Brooklands to the left and Westfield House on the right. The old West Wells Road on the left led to Runtlings Lane Junction (former Great Northern Railway) and Westfield Colliery. *Postcard.*

37. Runtlings Lane, looking towards Westfield Street, c.1935. At the head of the lane shown was Runtlings Lane Junction, where the railway forked to Chickenley Heath/Batley and Earlsheaton/Dewsbury. *Postcard: J E Shaw, Ossett.*

38. Healey Ferry in 1904, looking over the River Calder from the Healey (Ossett) side. The bearded boatman is pulling the craft across by applying his hands to a rope suspended from each bank. In 1906, a footbridge was constructed to replace the ferry. This, together with an improved bridleway made by Thornhill Urban District Council as far as the span bridge over the adjacent Calder & Hebble Navigation, improved access to and from Thornhill. *Postcard.*

39. Boatman's Cottage, Healey Ferry, 1904. This is also visible on the previous picture. The boatman is posed with his wife and family. The cottage grounds were quite extensive, with fruit trees, berry bushes and chickens. *Postcard.*

40. Wesley Street, Ossett, c.1940. To the left of the General Post Office is the shop of Samuel N Pickard, chemist. Beyond these buildings, the Methodist Chapel and schoolroom are partly visible. *Postcard.*

41. Wesley Street, c1908, showing, on the left, part of the premises occupied by Edward Clay & Son, then advertising as mungo manufacturers. The firm was established in 1870 by Edward Clay, first mayor of Ossett. The site had earlier formed part of Clegg's farm, the building with three pairs of windows being three farm cottages. *Postcard.*

42. Dewsbury Road at Streetside, Ossett. The tramcar, having emerged from Church Street, is travelling to Dewsbury. The shop on the right, now demolished, housed a sub-post office. The space at its side eventually formed part of Bridle Lane, leading to Gawthorpe. *Postcard: J E Shaw, Ossett.*

43. Crowds gathered in Ossett Market Place on 10 July 1912 to welcome King George V and Queen Mary. Here, the couple are being chauffeured along Dewsbury Road at Streetside for the next stage of their itinerary at Dewsbury. *Postcard.*

44. Kingsway, c.1960, before parts of the highway were narrowed and bollards fitted. Kingsway was opened on 21 August 1928 by Alderman G F Wilson. Several plots of land, through which the road would pass, were purchased by the Corporation during 1926 at prices ranging from £50 to £850. The town's other new road, Queen's Drive, was opened on 18 November 1926. *Photograph: N Ellis.*

45. The lower end of Kingsway and the Town Hall in late 1973. The Wilby & Crossland confectionery shop (formerly Griffin & Sayer) and Marianne's ladies fashion shop are shown already empty. They were demolished shortly after to extend Back Lane (now Ventnor Way) into Kingsway. The continuation of Ventnor Way along the back of the Co-op never got beyond the drawing board stage. *Photograph: N Ellis.*

46. In 1950, the executors of J H Glover gave land for the laying out of Broc-o-Dale Gardens on Kingsway. The old people's shelter on the extreme right was the gift of G Halmshaw. Its top half was eventually removed because of misuse. The picture dates from c.1955, when the gardens were well tended. *Postcard: F Frith, Reigate.*

47. Heath House, reached from Chancery Lane, is shown with an elegant conservatory and a variety of urn planters. The photograph is taken from a postcard which was used as a Christmas card. It was posted from Lily Wilson of Heath House to Miss Halstead of Highfields, Ossett, on 22 December 1904. *Postcard.*

48. In the 1730s, a school was founded in Ossett by the Society for Promoting Christian Knowledge. Successively called the Academy, Grammar School and Seminary, it was rebuilt in 1834 and reverted to the title of Ossett Grammar School. This illustration shows the school just before demolition in 1906 to make way for the Town Hall. Dale Street is on the left. In the interim period before moving to Park House, scholars were accommodated in the Baptist Sunday School on Church Street. *Photograph.*

49. In Gawthorpe, a school was built by public subscription in 1750, and rebuilt in 1811. This was located on the brow of Maypole Hill. It was replaced in 1840 by Gawthorpe Church of England School, situated at the junction of High Street and Leeds Road. This is shown on the composite picture, c.1925. It was superseded by the new Gawthorpe Council School, which opened on 30 May 1927. *Photograph.*

50. Park House and grounds at South Ossett were purchased by the Council to house the new Ossett Grammar School. The house, described as a Tudor Gothic mansion, had been built for Philip Ellis of Ellis Brothers, cloth manufacturers, in1867. Part of the crowd which assembled at Park House on opening day, 24 September 1906. is shown. The site was considered suitable to meet the needs of Ossett and Horbury. Girls and boys were admitted. *Postcard.*

51. The headmaster at the new Ossett Grammar School, until his retirement in 1913, was Mr M Frankland, who had been head at the old school. The number of pupils at the new school quickly leapt from an initial sixty. In 1914, arrangements were made to extend the premises, but these plans had to abandoned because of the war. In 1920 and 1924, wooden buildings were erected to cope with increased numbers. Since then, many changes and enlargements have been made. Following major refurbishment, the former Ossett Grammar School opened as Ossett School on 1 July 1970. Here, would-be cooks demonstrate their skills at the time. *Photograph.*

52. In 1814, the Vicar of Ossett, Rev Edward Kilvington, built a school in Old Church Street, near Ossett centre, in commemoration of peace after the Napoleonic Wars. It was used as a day and Sunday school until 1874, when Holy Trinity School was opened on Church Street. This was enlarged in 1895 and is pictured c.1920. *Postcard*.

53. South Ossett School was erected adjacent to Christ Church, South Ossett, in 1857. It was enlarged in 1894. Various aspects of the school are shown, c.1935, including 'physical jerks' in the playground. *Postcard: SS Photos, Blackpool.*

54. Southdale Council School on Southdale Road was opened on 22 August 1908 by Councillor J H Gibson, vice chairman of the Education Committee. It replaced the Wesleyan Day School in Wesley Street and catered for infants, girls and boys. The school forms a backdrop to this carnival float. *Postcard.*

55. Like the top picture, this photograph dates from between the 1914-18 and 1939-45 Wars. It shows the infants' entrance to Southdale School. Perhaps some of the boys were later called up for real army service. *Postcard.*

56. Holy Trinity Parish Church, Ossett, in 1904. The foundation stone was laid on Monday 30 June 1862. At 12.30 p.m., clergy of the diocese and other people assembled in and around the Grammar School in the Market Place. They processed to the site of the new edifice with the choir chanting the *Te Deum*. The procession included parishioners, children (around 300), the architect (William Henry Crossland), the builder (Matthew Hampshire) and the Bishop of Ripon. On arrival at the ground, the incumbent of Ossett, Rev Thomas Lee, said prayers, after which psalms and hymns were sung. Benjamin Ingham, then living in Sicily but formerly of Ossett, performed the ceremony of laying the stone. An ebony and silver mallet and a silver trowel were passed to him. In a cavity beneath the stone were placed a copy of the *Leeds Intelligencer* and various silver and copper coins for 1862. When the stone was lowered into place, Benjamin Ingham struck it three times and blessed it. A hymn was sung and the Bishop addressed the crowd. *Postcard.*

57. Holy Trinity Parish Church, c.1904, looking towards the chancel and east window. Opened in 1865, it replaced the earlier church in the Market Place. Benjamin Ingham, who laid the foundation stone in 1862, contributed £1,500 towards its erection, estimated at the time to be £8,500, excluding the cost of the ground. After the stone laying, Sunday school scholars were taken back to the old church, where each was presented with a currant bun and three pence. A luncheon was provided in the old church schoolroom for over two hundred people. In the evening, a soiree was held in the same location. This consisted of refreshments, speeches, solos and choral items. *Postcard.*

58. Holy Trinity Parish Church schoolfeast, 9 June 1909. Hats and caps have been donned for this annual gathering in front of the Town Hall. A few mortals have climbed the fountain. *Postcard.*

59. The Parish Church is shown electrically floodlit for a gift day on 23 May 1936. Note the time – ten minutes to midnight. *Postcard.*

60. Ranking high among Ossett's impressive buildings was the Wesleyan Methodist Chapel (often referred to as Church because of its size and splendour) on Wesley Street, built in 1866-68 and pictured here c.1904. The older chapel to its left, which opened in 1825, became a Sunday and day school. The original Methodist meeting place on this site dated from 1781. The buildings shown were demolished to make way for replacement buildings erected in 1963-64. These now serve Methodists and United Reformers. *Postcard.*

61. This interior shot of the Wesleyan Chapel on Wesley Street, with a fine looking organ and impressive pulpit, epitomises two great facets of Wesleyan Methodism – praising and preaching. BBC organist Reginald Foort once gave a recital on the organ on behalf of chapel funds. He afterwards autographed postcards of himself in front of an organ at a shilling a time, also for chapel coffers. *Postcard.*

Wesleyan School Room,
OSSETT.

The Ossett Choral Society have pleasure in announcing that they intend giving Mendelssohn's Grand Oratorio,

'ELIJAH,'

(For the first time in this neighbourhood), in the above School Room,

ON MONDAY EVENING, DEC. 13th, 1869,

The following eminent artistes have been engaged:—

Soprano: Miss AMY EMPSALL, Mrs LOFTHOUSE, and Mrs DOBSON;

Contralto: Mrs. LINCEY—NALTON;

Tenor: Mr SUTCLIFFE, of York Cathedral;

Basso: Mr JOSEPH CLAFTON, Oldham.

BAND:—FIRST VIOLIN, MR. BOWLING;
Second Violin, Mr P. S. Wilby;
VIOLA, MR. GLEDHILL;
Violoncellos, Messrs J. Pyrah and J. J. Mitchell;
Double Basses, Messrs Dearlove and J. Baxendale;
OBOE, MR. G. HARDING;
Flute, Mr George Crawshaw;
CLARIONETTE, MR. RICHARDSON;
Bassoon, Mr Northrop;
TRUMPET, MR. LOFTHOUSE;
Trombones, Messrs Jenkinson, Farrar and Laycock;
DRUMS, J. WAINWRIGHT, ESQ.;
Leader, Mr Bowling;
CONDUCTOR, MR. J. W. DEAN.

The Band and Chorus numbering about 70 performers.

Doors open at Seven, to commence at Half-past precisely.

Admission:—Reserved Seats, 3s.; Second Seats, 2s.; Third Seats, 1s. Tickets may be had of Mr J. Ellis, druggist; Mr R. Moore, Post-office; Mr W. Jenkinson, and at the door.

A Plan of the Reserved Seats may be seen on application to the Secretary, J. J. Mitchell.

BOOK OF WORDS 2d. EACH.

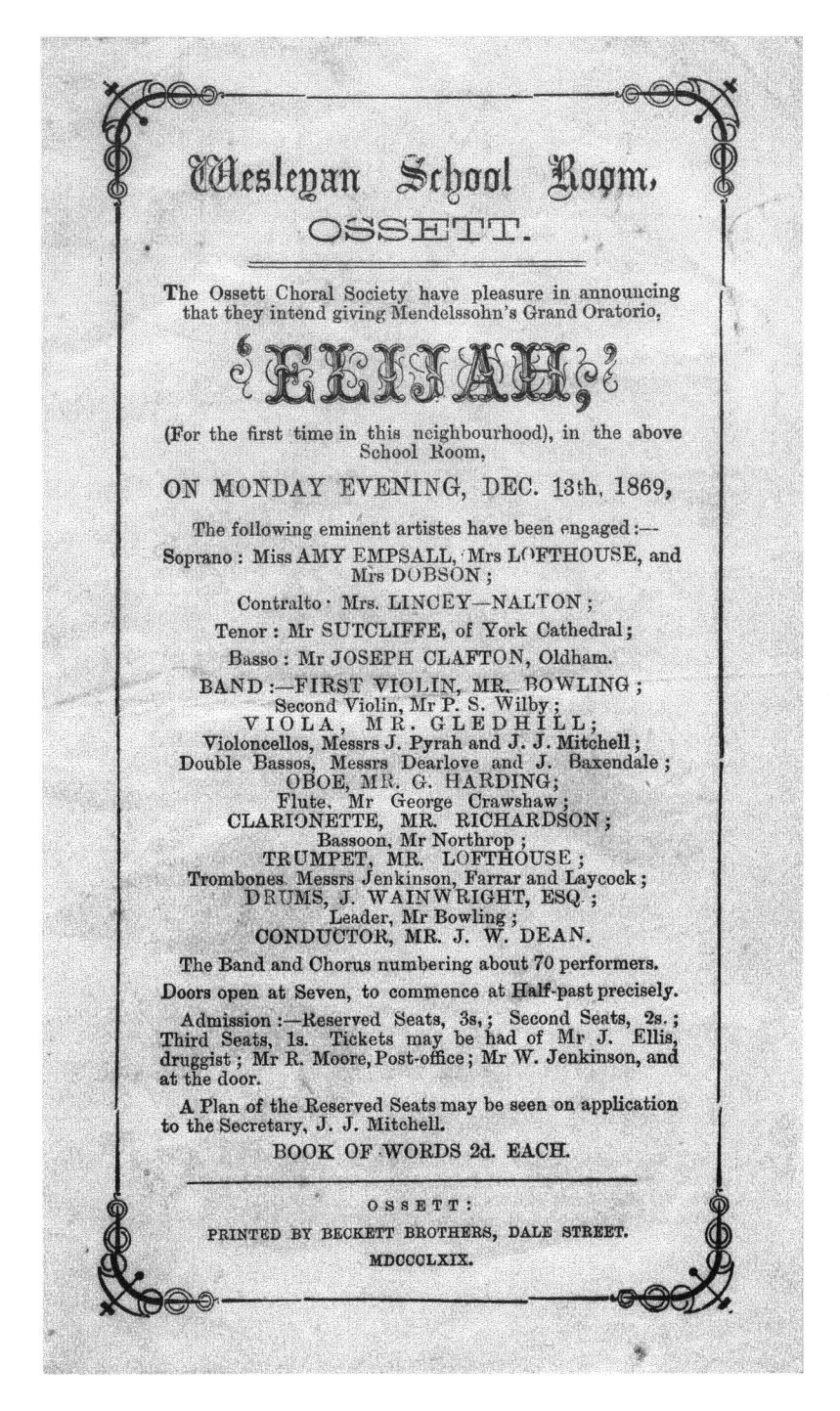

OSSETT:
PRINTED BY BECKETT BROTHERS, DALE STREET.
MDCCCLXIX.

62. Mendelssohn's oratorio *Elijah* was performed in the Wesleyan school room on 13 December 1869. Part of the school is visible on the upper picture of the previous page. The Book of Words, of which the front cover is shown above, was available to patrons. *Programme.*

63. The façade of the United Methodist Chapel (Church), built in 1895 to replace an 1857 structure, is pictured on Dale Street, c.1908. The word 'Free' was officially dropped from its title in 1907. It closed as a place of worship in 1964, the congregation transferring to the new Methodist Chapel (Church) on Wesley Street. Since then, the building has seen a variety of uses. *Postcard.*

64. The interior of the United Methodist Chapel on Dale Street, shown here, looks almost as impressive as its Wesleyan counterpart. As well as Sunday services, there were many ancillary activities, including a soccer club, formed from men who attended the bible class. A story is told that, when the club needed a new football, the committee asked the minister to contribute to the cost of £2. He gave the whole amount, but later took the money back because he was asked to pay at the door for one of the club's fundraising events. *Postcard: Norman C Gee, photographer, Ossett.*

Sunday school festival. Over four hundred persons took part in the annual festival of the Sunday school associated with the Methodist Free Church, Dale Street, which was held in delightful weather on Saturday. There was the customary procession through the streets, accompanied by the Borough Brass Band, and led by the Rev F E Watts, circuit minister, and Mr George Dews, school superintendent. The route paraded was along Dale Street, Dewsbury Road and along Springstone Avenue to Ryecroft Street, where, under the direction of Mr Blakeley Ellis, several of the festival hymns were sung. The singing was afterwards repeated at the residence, in Church Street, of Mr Joseph Ellis, an aged member of the Church, who is ill. The procession then proceeded along Dale Street and Town End, stopping and singing on the site of the old chapel, along Prospect Road and Station Road to the Market Place, where the singing was concluded. Tea was served in the school, and the evening spent in games etc in the Gedham Field (lent by the Co-operative Society) where the band also rendered musical selections. ***Ossett Observer***, *7 July 1906.*

Evangelical mission. The evangelistic mission commenced last week at the United Methodist Free Church, Dale Street, by Sister Monica of Bowron House, London, was concluded last evening. Weeknight services have been held during the past fortnight, being numerously attended, and several converts have been made. A midnight mission took place on Saturday. Workers assembled in the Market Place about half past ten o'clock and, after a short meeting, walked in procession through the streets singing hymns and calling at various public houses, where an invitation was given to the company to attend the service being held in the schoolroom. It consisted of prayers, hymn singing and addresses by Sister Monica, the Rev F E Watts and Mr Westerman, Wesleyan town missionary. The service was of a hearty character and concluded about half past twelve. On Thursday evening, Sister Monica gave a lecture describing the object and work of the Bowron House Sisterhood and her own experiences as a missionary, the lecture being very interesting. At several of the meetings, solos were sung be Sister Monica and members of the choir. ***Ossett Observer***, *10 September 1906.*

65. United Methodist Chapel schoolfeast gathering at Ossett Market Place in 1911, with hymn sheets at the ready. Schoolfeasts and Sunday school anniversaries were usually held at or about Whitsuntide, when children were allowed to wear their new clothes. For the girls, this often meant white frocks, which are in evidence here. The tramcar is poised ready for its return journey to Wakefield and Agbrigg. *Postcard.*

66. The Baptist Chapel on Church Street, also used as a Sunday school, was used for worship until 1973, later becoming part of the RGS Pattern Book Company. The doctors' surgery was built in front of the chapel. *Photograph: N Ellis.*

67. The banner, near the Town Hall, declares that this is a Queen Street Primitive Methodist Sunday School celebration, probably a schoolfeast, in the early 1900s. The 'Prims' loved their rousing tuneful hymns, one of the favourites being *The Lion of Judah* set to an old chartist tune. *Postcard: Thomas Crawshaw & Son, linen drapers and booksellers, 12 Market Place, Ossett.*

68. The stars of this production at the Primitive Methodist Chapel at South Parade in 1926 included Mary Driver, Florence Grace and Lilian Townend. The cast is featured outside the chapel, with Clarence Richmond, the producer, on the extreme right. He kept a fish and chip shop on Bank Street. *Postcard.*

69. The Green Congregational Chapel (Church), c.1906. It opened in 1883, replacing an earlier edifice of 1850, demolished in 1882. Designed to hold 1,008 adults, the architect claimed that, with the usual proportion of children, 1,200 persons could be seated. The building, handsome both externally and internally, incorporated a spire that rose to 122 feet above road level and was a landmark in the vicinity. Beyond the chapel is the school building of 1864. The congregation had to move to the former Primitive Methodist school room on Queen's Terrace in 1973, at the same time becoming part of the newly-formed United Reformed Church (an amalgamation of the Congregational and Presbyterian Churches). *Postcard: H G Glen & Co, Leeds.*

70. The Green Congregational Chapel. The back of this card, sent by Edith (postmarked Ossett, 25 April 1906) to Miss Ada Booth of Horbury Road, Ossett, includes the message, *"Please can you go somewhere with me tonight. Meet me by Green Chapel no later than 7"*. Postcard.

Garden party. A garden party, promoted in connection with the Congregational Church, The Green, for the benefit of the funds of the London Missionary Society, took place on Saturday, in the grounds of Grange View, the residence of Mr J W Smith. The weather was delightful and the gathering was largely attended. Tea was served on the lawn by lady members of the missionary committee, about two hundred persons partaking. The adjoining grounds of Mr Eli Townend and his natural history museum were also thrown open to the visitors, a privilege which was greatly appreciated. Various games were enjoyed, and much amusement caused by a cricket match between ladies and gentlemen. A needlework stall, at which good business was done, was looked after by Mesdames Otty, J S Wilby, A Westerman, John Pollard, R C Saberton and J A Rusby. The proceeds, including the receipts from the stall, amounted to the satisfactory sum of £11. ***Ossett Observer, 23 June 1906.***

71. This Wesleyan Methodist Chapel on South Parade was built in 1846, with a schoolroom below, a design which obviously saved money. It is seen here c.1905. A new replacement chapel to seat about 400 persons was erected in 1908 to a then modern design by architects Garside & Pennington of Pontefract and Castleford. *Postcard.*

72. An unidentified event, but almost certainly another church or chapel schoolfeast gathering, is pictured in Ossett Market Place, with Cox Brothers' ironmongery shop in the centre background and Station Road on the right. A row of long-demolished houses is partly visible on the left. The umbrellas are keeping off the sun. *Postcard.*

73. Pildacre Colliery was frequently troubled by water; severe flooding in 1911 made coal production impossible. In 1922, Ossett Council decided to tap this vast underground source of water to provide the town's supply. Previously, water had come from a service reservoir at Staincliffe which belonged to the Dewsbury & Heckmondwike Waterworks Board. The water had been pumped through three miles of cast iron pipe to a storage reservoir at Gawthorpe, capable of holding one million gallons. The new scheme involved erection of the water tower at Gawthorpe and construction of waterworks at Pildacre. The treated water would be passed along 1 ½ miles of pipe to the tower. The work, which included negotiations with the Great Northern Railway, was fully completed in 1928. The concrete tower at Gawthorpe, 150 feet high, is pictured at about the time of its formal inauguration on 12 February 1925. The foundation stone for the Pildacre Waterworks was laid on the same day; these were opened on 21 February 1928. *Postcard: Norman C Gee, Ossett.*

74. This begrimed scene shows Old Roundwood Colliery, c.1908, with part of the brickworks on the right. The colliery originated in the early 1850s. By 1862, a railway, which crossed Dewsbury Road, and increasingly held up road traffic in its later days, linked the pit with the Great Northern Railway at Low Laithes. On 20 June 1888, three sinkers were being lowered down a new 200 feet deep shaft, when the bucket they were in capsized 40 feet from the bottom. Matthew Harrison of Ashton-under-Lyne and George Geary of Wakefield were killed by the fall. In 1893, new screens were erected, only to be destroyed shortly after by an extensive fire. Through subsequent years, strikes and wage disputes caused further disruption, but the colliery survived until 1966. *Postcard.*

75. After arriving home from a shift, colliers stripped to the waist and removed as much muck as possible at the kitchen sink. Perhaps once a week, before houses had bathrooms, the tin bath was brought out and filled with hot water. By the 1920s, pithead baths were starting to appear. This illustration from 1933 shows the new baths at Old Roundwood Colliery. *Photograph.*

76. When Shaw Cross Colliery closed in 1968, coal had been mined in the Ossett area for about 700 years. The early mines were primitive bell pits. Shaw Cross Colliery was just over the Ossett boundary in Dewsbury, but had workings under Ossett and employed many Ossett men. It was served by the Chickenley Heath railway line. The pit was sunk in 1903. This picture dates from the time of its closure. The spire of Holy Trinity Parish Church, Ossett, is visible on the horizon.
Photograph: courtesy Tony Banks, Kirkhamgate.

77. Walter Ashton was born in Wakefield where he became apprenticed to a wheelwright. After marrying in 1889, he and his wife moved to Ossett in 1890, where he established a wheelwright's business on Prospect Road. He is seen outside his wheelwright's shop, with the Green Congregational Chapel visible on the right. *Photograph: E I Walker, photographer, Castleford, courtesy Muriel Wood, Ossett.*

78. Walter Ashton branched into vehicle body building, with premises on Bank Street, near the site of 'Little Monsters'. The newly painted bodywork shown was made from blue prints. It was lowered on to a Leyland chassis which had been delivered to the workshop, the new vehicle being for Langley Brothers, mungo manufacturers of Dale Street. Walter is pictured at the right of the group. His son, Ernest, who became a sign writer, is leaning from the cab window. Three of Walter's sons worked in the family business. After his wife died, Walter retired and moved to a small house in Church Street. *Photograph: courtesy Muriel Wood, Ossett.*

79. Walter Ashton had five sons and one daughter. The Ashtons built wagons, carts and wheelbarrows for the Co-op, Langley's mill and other local firms. However, eldest son Charles went into butchering and is pictured outside James Hampshire Nettleton's shop in Wesley Street, now 'Rhythm & Booze'. *Photograph: courtesy Muriel Wood, Ossett.*

80. The Sutcliffe Moulded Rubber Company came into existence in 1947 at Ashbrook House, Church Street, Ossett. The property consisted of one large house, a warehouse and a billiard room, plus 2 ½ acres of land with stabling facilities. The firm, which specialised in rubber-to-metal bonded components for industry, expanded on the site, the above factory dating from 1950 onwards. Much of the location is now covered by the residential Ashbrook Close, although Ashbrook House remains. *Photograph.*

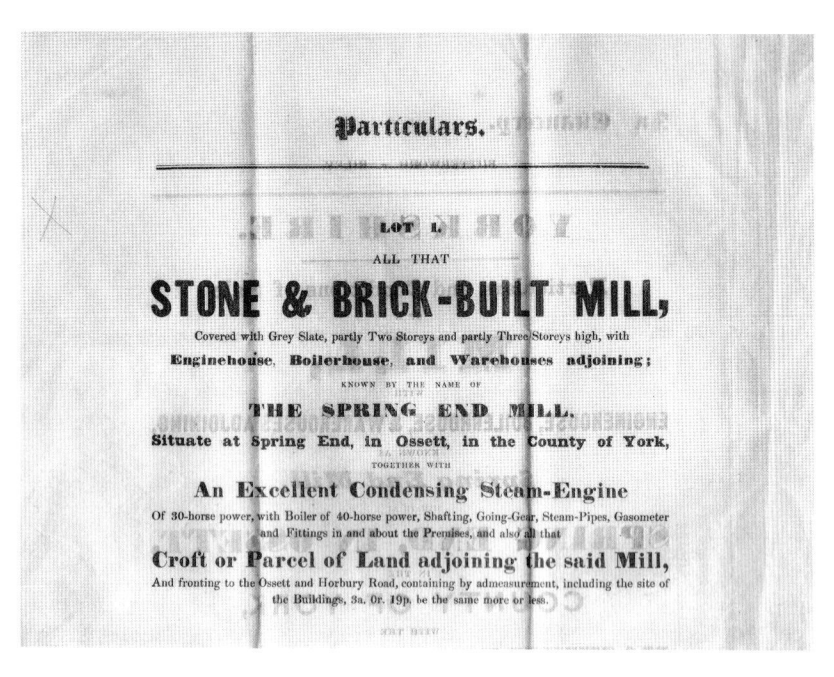

Particulars.

LOT 1.

ALL THAT

STONE & BRICK-BUILT MILL,

Covered with Grey Slate, partly Two Storeys and partly Three Storeys high, with

Enginehouse, Boilerhouse, and Warehouses adjoining;

KNOWN BY THE NAME OF

THE SPRING END MILL.

Situate at Spring End, in Ossett, in the County of York,

TOGETHER WITH

An Excellent Condensing Steam-Engine

Of 30-horse power, with Boiler of 40-horse power, Shafting, Going-Gear, Steam-Pipes, Gasometer and Fittings in and about the Premises, and also all that

Croft or Parcel of Land adjoining the said Mill,

And fronting to the Ossett and Horbury Road, containing by admeasurement, including the site of the Buildings, 3a. 0r. 19p, be the same more or less.

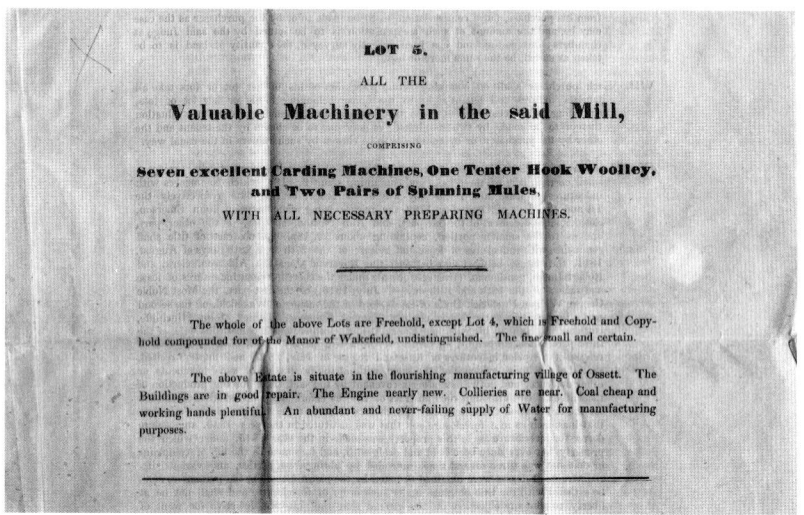

LOT 5.

ALL THE

Valuable Machinery in the said Mill,

COMPRISING

Seven excellent Carding Machines, One Tenter Hook Woolley, and Two Pairs of Spinning Mules,

WITH ALL NECESSARY PREPARING MACHINES.

The whole of the above Lots are Freehold, except Lot 4, which is Freehold and Copyhold compounded for of the Manor of Wakefield, undistinguished. The fine small and certain.

The above Estate is situate in the flourishing manufacturing village of Ossett. The Buildings are in good repair. The Engine nearly new. Collieries are near. Coal cheap and working hands plentiful. An abundant and never-failing supply of Water for manufacturing purposes.

81a, 81b. These are extracts from the prospectus of a sale by auction (in chancery) to be held at the Fleece Inn, Ossett Low Common, on Thursday 25 September 1856 at 6.00 p.m. The estate at Spring End, Ossett, was divided into five lots: lot 1 - the mill; lot 2 - a 3 acre close of land on the Ossett and Horbury Road; lot 3 - the Fleece Inn; lot 4 - a 2 acre field of arable land; lot 5 - valuable machinery in the said mill. Nevertheless, lots 1 and 5 (above) were sold by private treaty for £1,000 and £800 respectively to James Marchent of Bradford on 22 January 1857. The final paragraph for lot 5 paints a glowing picture of the estate and *"the flourishing manufacturing village (sic) of Ossett"*. *Prospectus.*

82. Fred Firth, later known as Firth (Ossett) Ltd, oil extractors and mungo manufacturers, occupied Pale Side Works and Mill on Dewsbury Road at Paleside. The illustration is from a billhead used in 1905. *Billhead.*

83. Fawcett & Firth were proprietors of Calder Vale Mills at Healey, where mungo and shoddy were produced. Their lorry, with barrels containing collected urine, is shown parked beside Wheatroyd Terrace on Healey Road, with driver Tom Robinson. Urine was used in the scouring (cleaning) of wool, the active ingredient being ammonia. Namesake Tony Robinson, of television fame, might consider urine handling to be one of 'the worst jobs in history', although night soil removal was worse. *Postcard.*

84. The Ossett Industrial Co-operative Society was formed in 1861, the main buildings on Dale Street being opened in 1873 and 1884. Adjoining properties were absorbed later and several branches were opened. The 'divi' paper check system was replaced by stamps. Here, in 1988, a wide range of departments is visible, comprising (left to right) electrical, homewares, confectionery, grocery, outfitting, fish/fruit and footwear. Not visible are the furniture, carpet and butchering departments. A bakery was situated at the rear. *Photograph.*

85. Ossett Co-op closed down on Saturday 10 April 1993. In early 1997, plans were announced to demolish the buildings and construct new ones, largely using the same stone. This demolition scene was captured in late 1997. The new Co-op store opened on Monday 21 September 1998. It incorporates a supermarket, travel agency and chemist, also a housing complex. *Photograph: N Ellis.*

86. Hillards in Ossett was on the site of the Palladium Cinema, until the move to this purpose-built store on Bank Street, pictured here in 1988. It briefly became Tesco and is now the site of 'Little Monsters'. Popular lines such as coffee, tea bags and Jaffa cakes are advertised in the window. *Photograph.*

87. The Shaw Peace, stationers, premises in Wesley Street are shown shortly before closure and demolition. The notice board of the new Methodist Chapel on the left is advertising a Christmas Fayre for 17 November 1973. A footpath ran between these two buildings into Kingsway. *Photograph: N Ellis.*

88. Ossett Gas Company was formed in 1854. The gas works on Healey Road were taken over by the Corporation in 1901. The gas industry was nationalised in 1949, when the Ossett undertaking became vested in the North Eastern Gas Board. This group of workmen is believed to be assembled on Back Lane. The man in the white apron is Mr Carter, one time chairman of Ossett Town Football Club, who lived on Field Lane. *Postcard.*

89. The carnival float for Ossett Corporation's gas department carries various gas appliances; also a fine motor horn. The appliances could be purchased from the department's shop on Station Road. *Postcard.*

90. Jonas Woodhead & Sons, Kirkstall Road, Leeds, with almost a century of design and manufacture of road and rail springs behind them, purchased premises in Ossett known as Moorcroft Mills in 1948. These works, off Church Street, were originally built for Hepworth Brothers, mungo rag merchants. Following the outbreak of war in 1939, the mill was commandeered by the Ministry of Aircraft Production and used by a branch of Rotol to make airscrews. After the war, it was leased to Airmec, a subsidiary of Philco, for the assembly of wireless sets. Jonas Woodhead arrived in 1948. Plant was quickly installed for the manufacture of coil springs for road vehicle suspensions. This was immediately followed by installation of equipment for producing Monroe hydraulic shock absorbers, which had been developed in America by Monroe Auto Equipment Company. The shock absorber section was named Woodhead Monroe, later becoming Woodhead Manufacturing Company. The above picture, although lacking in clarity, shows the extent of the Woodhead works in 1970. Church Street is in the lower right corner. The older parts of the factory run diagonally at the right, with newer extensions towards the left. The gable-ended building to right of bottom centre is Northfield Mill, acquired by Woodhead in about 1960 from Bickle Brothers, rag merchants, mungo manufacturers, carbonizers and dyers. A series of setbacks in the 1990s led to Woodhead's final demise, although the smaller coil spring section had disappeared some years earlier. Most of the site is now covered with houses and apartments, although Northfield Mill and its gatehouse remain. *Photograph.*

91. This photograph shows construction work at the Hepworth Brothers Moorcroft Mills, probably c.1920. The contractor was M Senior. The building, shown nearing completion, was probably used for receiving and despatching goods. The spire of the Parish Church is in the background.
Postcard: Norman C Gee, Ossett.

92. Various types of Woodhead shock absorbers are shown on a display board, including conventional dampers, Kingsway Struts and Loadmasters. Miss Woodhead 1978 adds a touch of glamour. *Photograph.*

93. In addition to the serious business of working, many Woodhead employees were involved in the activities of the Sports & Social Club. There were excursions to the races or the seaside, including children's trips, plus an annual dinner dance. For many years, decorated floats were entered in the Gawthorpe Maypole procession and other events. The above picture includes the trophies won with floats at Birkenshaw Show, Elland Charity Carnival and Halifax Charity Gala. Some of those posing with Miss Woodhead 1971 are Harold Firth (left), Iris Massingham (centre) and Alf Reynolds (right). *Photograph.*

94. This is the Woodhead float for 1969 at the Gawthorpe Maypole Procession. Its theme was the Aztecs. This was submitted by the Sports & Social Club. In front can be seen the float entered by the Company, with mock shock absorbers supporting a globe of the earth, incorporating 13,000 hand-made paper flowers. Woodhead workpeople were responsible for the hard graft of making both these displays. *Photograph: N Ellis.*

95. This float, exhibited by the Woodhead Company in 1971, is featured at Gawthorpe. The fiend in front actually represents a suspension damper and a laminated spring, while there are shock absorber replicas at either side of the wagon. *Photograph: N Ellis.*

96. Northfield Mill on Church Street was gutted by fire in October 1888, Abraham Pollard, head of John Speight & Sons, mungo manufacturers, had purchased the mill earlier in the year. It was quickly rebuilt and commenced production again in 1889. By the 1920s, the mill belonged to Bickle Brothers. It was purchased by the adjacently-sited Woodhead Monroe in July 1960, eventually housing the development department and various offices. At around midnight on Saturday 11 July 1987, the fire alarm was raised (detailed in the preface). This shot of the rear of the mill was taken just after the fire. The car park was once the site of the mill pond. Internal damage was severe. *Photograph: N Ellis.*

97. Northfield Mill from Church Street in July 1987, showing more fire damage to the roof. The date of the rebuild, 1888, and the name of the mill are visible above the entrance. *Photograph: N Ellis.*

98. Woodhead employees in hard hats survey some of the fire and water damage to the upper storey of Northfield Mill on the morning of Sunday 12 July 1987. The suspended ceiling looks particularly bad. *Photograph: N Ellis.*

99. On Monday morning, 13 July, sodden tiles and carpets were removed from the offices of Northfield Mill and laid out to dry on the ground or walls outside, as shown. The house in the background was once the home of Sam Bickle. It became the property of Zenith Security. *Photograph: N Ellis.*

100. It soon became obvious that a big salvage operation was necessary after the Woodhead fire. As much as possible was rescued, some items being temporarily placed outside the affected building, which is visible in the background.. *Photograph: N Ellis.*

101. More office furniture and files! Employees who worked in Northfield Mill were found alternative accommodation within a few days, some of them ending up in the canteen building at the Kingsway end, which was no longer used to provide meals. A lot of the equipment and furniture was a write-off, but as much paperwork as possible was saved. The building in the background (behind the lorry and trailer) was one of the later additions to the Woodhead complex. The entrance to the reception area is partly visible on the left. *Photograph: N Ellis.*

Colliery Trip. The annual excursion organised in connection with the accident fund of the Old Roundwood Collieries took place on Saturday to Bridlington. About five hundred persons took the opportunity of visiting the seaside, travelling by two special GNR trains, the first of which left Ossett at a quarter to six o'clock in the morning and the second an hour later. Bridlington was reached after about a three hours' run. The weather was delightfully fine, and the day was enjoyably spent. The town was gaily decorated, and during the day some of the proceedings in connection with the new Spa pavilion were continued. These included a procession of civic and other representatives. A number of the trippers also visited Flamborough Head, walking along the cliffs. The return journey was begun about a quarter to ten at night, Ossett being reached about one o'clock on Sunday morning. ***Ossett Observer,*** *14 July 1906.*

Workpeople's trip. Several local business firms provided their employees with excursions to the seaside on Saturday, among them being Messrs Langley Brothers Ltd, mungo manufacturers, Dale Street (86 excursionists); Hanson & Wormald Ltd, mungo manufacturers, Royds Mill, Gawthorpe (70); and Wilson Brothers, mungo manufacturers, Chickenley Mills (80). Special GNR trains ran to Bridlington, Filey and Scarborough, most of the trippers going to the first named place. The weather was pleasantly fine and the visitors thoroughly enjoyed themselves. The return railway journey was accomplished about half past eleven at night. ***Ossett Observer,*** *28 July 1906.*

Tramcar and wagon in collision. A tramcar and a mineral water wagon collided at the corner of Prospect Road and Station Road on Monday evening. The tramcar was approaching the Market Place at the same time as the wagon, drawn by two horses, was being driven in the direction of Mr Pickard's shop, near to which they met. The driver of the wagon attempted to avert the collision by drawing his horses across the road, and he almost succeeded, the only damage being that the pole of the wagon was broken. Luckily, the horses remained calm, showing not the least signs of restiveness, or considerable injury might have been caused. ***Ossett Observer,*** *15 September 1906.*

102. The Bradford, Wakefield & Leeds Railway Company opened a branch line from Wrenthorpe to Flushdyke in 1862, which was extended to Ossett and Batley in 1864. The first Ossett Station was reached from the Market Place via New Street. The Bradford, Wakefield & Leeds Railway was soon absorbed by the Great Northern Railway Company. A line from Runtlings Lane Junction to Dewsbury, via Earlsheaton, was added in 1874. A new Ossett Station was opened slightly further west in 1889, in conjunction with the construction of Station Road. Ossett thus acquired rail connections with Dewsbury, Batley and Wakefield – and further afield. The new Ossett Station is pictured above, looking towards The Green, c.1910. The spire of the Congregational Chapel and the roof of Southdale School can be made out. The station's long island platform had tracks at each side. Those in the foreground ran to the goods warehouse on the east side of Station Road. The thriving mungo and shoddy trade necessitated a large station and goods yard. Up until the 1960s, the station witnessed special trains leaving for seaside excursions, club trips and Rugby League matches. Following the Beeching Report, the station and goods yard were closed in 1964 and houses built on the site. *Postcard: William Colin Machan, fancy goods dealer, Wakefield.*

103. Flushdyke's first station was opened in 1862 on the north side of the Wakefield to Dewsbury Road. After the line was extended to Ossett and Batley in 1864, a new station was opened on the opposite side of the road; it is seen here, c.1910, looking in the direction of Wakefield. Flushdyke Station closed in 1941, although the line was used into the middle 1960s. The simple station had an elevated position on an embankment. The timber platforms look very clean – had a porter been out with his sweeping brush? *Postcard: H M Wilson, photographer, Wood Street, Wakefield.*

104. A GNR motor train is seen resting at the single platform of Chickenley Heath Station. This was opened in 1877, but was closed to passengers in 1909 because of competition from Ossett to Dewsbury trams, which stopped near the station. The line continued in use for mineral traffic. The inclined path on the right lead down from the roadside booking office. This building found use as a mission hall in the late 1950s, but was demolished along with the nearby Station Hotel when the Ossett bypass was constructed. *Postcard.*

105. Simmering in the sidings near Ossett Station is one of the steam rail motor trains introduced on the line from Ossett to Batley, via Chickenley Heath, in February 1906. The Great Northern Railway had already used these on the other Ossett and Batley branch, via Earlsheaton and Dewsbury. The integral locomotive and carriage were mounted on a single frame. *Postcard.*

106. The tramway passenger service from Agbrigg to Ossett, via Wakefield and Horbury, was launched on 15 August 1904. The inaugural tram, number 16, belonging to the Yorkshire (West Riding) Electric Tramways Company, is seen emerging from the end of Station Road into Bank Street. The terminus was moved nearer to the Town Hall in 1908, to share a common loop with trams from Dewsbury. *Postcard.*

107. A West Riding tramcar is featured outside the WR depot at Sowood Lane, Ossett. New in 1905, it was built complete with top cover. Trams which were built for the company with open upper decks were later given top covers. The destination indicator is set at Leeds, but this was on another route operated by the same concern. The company's main depot was at Belle Isle, Wakefield. *Postcard.*

108. On Saturday 31 May 1929, this specially decorated West Riding tramcar was photographed in Ossett Market Place with civic dignitaries and others, including the Mayor, Councillor Numa Armitage. The League of Nations was an international organisation created after the 1914-18 War to secure world peace. It failed in this objective. *Postcard.*

109. The depot for the Dewsbury & Ossett Tramways (originally called the Dewsbury, Ossett & Soothill Nether Tramways) was erected in Church Street, Ossett. Adjacent to it was the Yorkshire Electric Power Company sub-station, from which the D&O obtained power. The illustration comes from the early 1930s, by which time the tramcars, which were built with open upper decks, had received top covers. On the back row, left, under the destination sign is Mr Shadlock, a motorman (driver). The group of workpeople also includes Messrs B Audsley, T Bragg, L Farnhill, H Gothard, H Jackson, P Newsome, H Noble, D Stones, E Sugden, B Willans and Mrs Senior. *Postcard.*

110. The rear of the Town Hall in 1973, photographed from the car park and showing the bus station, whose days were then numbered. Since the time of the trams, buses had used a range of terminal points near the Town Hall. *Photograph: N Ellis.*

111. Bus station construction in late 1973, with the former Methodist Chapel, Parish Church and Fire Station in the background. During construction of the current bus station, partly on the site shown above, temporary stops were positioned along Prospect Road, near the football ground. The new bus station was opened in August 2005. *Photograph: N Ellis.*

112. The circus comes to Ossett! Sanger's Circus is seen passing along Station Road, near The Gables, in May 1904, with an anticipatory throng in pursuit. *Postcard.*

113. The Palladium Cinema, Market Place, Ossett. Built facing the east side of the Town Hall, it opened on 22 December 1913 with the silent film *Greater Love Hath No Man*. The Palladium's orchestra accompanied the silent films. These gave way to sound films, but the curtain descended for the last time on 29 April 1961, with a performance of *The Miracle*. The cinema was demolished in March 1962. *Postcard.*

114. The cricket ground and pavilion, Radley Street, Ossett, c.1907. The railway embankment is visible in the background. At the time, the many cricket teams in the area included Ossett, Chickenley, Old Roundwood Colliery, Ossett Primitive Methodist, Ossett Wesleyan, Ossett Temperance, Flushdyke Bethel and South Ossett Church Institute. *Postcard.*

115. Members of the Ossett Borough Prize Band, with instruments and shoes shining, pose before the cricket pavilion, off Radley Street, in 1923. *Postcard: Fred Hartley, photographer, Dewsbury.*

116. This float, entered in one of the Ossett Hospital & Convalescent Association carnival processions, has won a second prize. It is standing on Dewsbury Road, near the end of Springstone Avenue. *Postcard: Norman C Gee, Ossett.*

117. The Gawthorpe Victoria Brass Band in 1910. John Paley, the conductor from 1903 to 1911, is seated in the centre behind the drum. John had been cornet soloist for Black Dyke and other bands. This card was posted to chimney sweep William Garside of Giggal Hill, South Ossett, with a request to sweep two chimneys for Mrs E Squires of Croft Cottage, Broadhead's Yard, Gawthorpe. *Postcard.*

Success of local brass band. The Gawthorpe Victoria Brass Band, conducted by Mr J Paley, carried off the premier honours in a brass band contest at the Bridge Pleasure Grounds, Ilkley, on Easter Monday. Mr J W Beswick of Manchester was the judge, and the test piece was the now popular selection, *Carmelite,* by Cope. Seventeen bands competed. Gawthorpe were awarded the first prize, £8 in cash, and the Iles Silver Challenge Cup. Scapegoat Hill obtained the second prize, Birstall Old third and Barrow Iron & Steel Works fourth. The Gawthorpe band also competed against twelve other bands at a contest held at Brierfield on Saturday, but was not included among the prize winners. ***Ossett Observer,*** *21 April 1906.*

The feast. The annual festivity known as Ossett Feast took place last weekend, the Gedham field being for three or four days the centre of much noise and activity. In addition to the usual shooting galleries, 'Aunt Sallies', shooting booths, temporary theatres and various side shows, one or two novelties were this year introduced, including a tower, encircling which was a sort of toboggan slide, down which daring spirits descended at considerable speed while seated on a mat – often to their discomfort and no little laughter – while an enterprising roundabout proprietor had pressed the motor car into service, in place of the old-fashioned 'hobby horses'. During the weekend, the feast ground was thronged nightly, and business from the attraction proprietors' point of view appeared to be exceedingly satisfactory. ***Ossett Observer,*** *16 June 1906.*

Temperance meeting at the feast. The Ossett Temperance Society, following an old practice, held its meetings on Sunday afternoon and evening in the feast ground, where large audiences assembled. The proprietor of one of the shows kindly placed the platform of his establishment at the society's disposal, a privilege which was greatly appreciated. Mr Herbert Smith officiated as chairman, and excellent addresses in advocacy of the temperance cause were delivered by Mr E J Johnson of Derby. At the evening meeting, duets were tastefully sung by Miss S Brook and Mr B Wilby, and Mrs J Teale and Mrs W Naylor. ***Ossett Observer,*** *16 June 1906.*

118. Following the Peace Proclamation on 19 July 1919, children of the Borough were entertained to tea in the Town Hall and Southdale School, plus other locations. Afterwards, there were sports and entertainments in Gedham. This huge bonfire was lit and a brilliant display of fireworks was provided. On 21 July, soldiers and sailors on leave, and those demobilised, plus wives and lady friends, and widows and mothers of those who had fallen, were entertained to tea in the Town Hall and Southdale School. Later, a concert was put on in the Town Hall. On 22 July, all residents of the Borough of sixty years of age and upwards were provided with tea in the Town Hall and Southdale School. A concert was laid on in the Town Hall. On each of the three days, the Ossett Borough and Gawthorpe Victoria Prize Bands played selections. Total cost for the three days was £1,139, defrayed by public subscription. *Postcard.*

119. Believed to be 1928, this picture shows the Ossett 'Raggers' and others on a Friday evening outside the Cock & Bottle Hotel in the Market Place. The message on the back of the card reads: *"The tower which is covered here was unveiled at 9 o'clock and a rocket went up into the sky with such a bang everybody was wondering whatever was going to happen"*. Observe the dressed-up characters in the centre of the photo. *Postcard.*

120. Again thought to be 1928 or thereabout, the Ossett 'Raggers' procession is captured parading down Station Road with scouts and cubs in the foreground and decorated floats behind. *Postcard.*

121. In about 1936, Councillor Robert H Wilby became associated with the Ossett Hospital & Convalescent Association. His main contribution was writing and producing a series of outdoor reviews. His first, in association with Fred Littlewood and others was *Ossett Calling*. This was followed in 1937 by *All Tahns Tawkin*. In 1938, the production was *High Societe*. Only one of the three performances of this was held in the gala field off Queen's Drive, the others being held in the Town Hall due to rain. Part of the cast for *High Societe* is shown. It includes Ella Thompson, Muriel Tetley, Betty Forrest, Florence Lodge, Gladys Fisher, Jessie Dews, Dorothy Pawson, Margaret Horsfield and Winnie Fawcett. *Postcard.*

122. The Ossett Common Carnival Queen, Eileen Ashton, and her retinue in 1937. *Postcard.*

123. Gawthorpe is renowned for its maypole celebrations which date back to the 1850s or even earlier. The unique coal carrying race was begun in 1963. The above panorama of the centre of Gawthorpe shows maypole plaiting, stalls and gipsy-type caravans around 1908. Legends exist about some of the early Gawthorpe maypoles. It is said that the neighbouring Streetsiders (or was it the Chickenleyites?) were jealous of one maypole, which had a large wooden cockerel at the top to indicate the direction of the wind. One dark night, they attempted to saw it down but were disturbed. A fight ensued with the Gawthorpers, until some of the womenfolk intervened. Soon after, a gale toppled the crippled pole to the ground. *Postcard.*

124. 'John Bull' attracts attention at the Gawthorpe Maypole celebrations on 6 May 1911. *Postcard: Fred Hartley, Dewsbury.*

125. The Ossett ambulance moves along Dewsbury Road in the Gawthorpe Maypole procession, c.1910. The course of the parade, starting in Gawthorpe, was down 'Benny Harrop Hill' and High Street and on to the Chickenley Heath boundary, then back along Streetside and down Church Street into Ossett (Kingsway came later). A halt was made in the Market Place where the band played. The return was via Illingworth Street, Queen Street, Bank Street, Dale Street, Dewsbury Road and Owl Lane as far as the boundary, then back to Gawthorpe. Over the years, minor deviations have been made, with Kingsway becoming the norm for the outward journey. *Postcard.*

126. This horse-drawn float was entered in the 1911 Gawthorpe Maypole procession. At that time, the equestrian content of the event was strong. *Postcard: Fred Hartley, Dewsbury.*

127. The Gawthorpe Maypole procession, 2 May 1970, showing the entry from the Sunday school of St Mary's Parish Church, Gawthorpe, now closed. The parade was led by the Ossett & Gawthorpe Friendly Prize Band. Other participants included the horse-drawn Tetley's Brewery wagon and a pony-pulled Rington's Tea van. *Photograph: N Ellis.*

128. Having returned up Church Street, the 1970 Gawthorpe procession passes the Flying Horse and proceeds along Dewsbury Road, with the Mayor and Mayoress in the front car. *Photograph: N Ellis.*

129. The Ossett War Memorial was erected in the centre of Kingsway, facing the side of the Town Hall. Preceded by a procession, it was unveiled, as shown, on the afternoon of Armistice Sunday, 11 November 1928, by the Right Honourable the Lord Viscount Lascelles. The crowd that attended included relatives of the fallen, various uniformed and other organisations, and the general public. A plan had been prepared to indicate where everyone must stand. *Postcard.*

130. Here, Lord Lascelles is speaking after the unveiling. The Mayor, Councillor Numa Armitage, is to his left. The singing of hymns, including *For all the saints,* was accompanied by the Ossett Military Band. As the umbrellas indicate, the weather was inclement. The memorial was designed by Mr H Holmes, Ossett's borough surveyor, and Mr C Kendall, architect. The bronze figure, a life-sized figure of a soldier (not on the picture), was the work of Mr R Lindsay Clark, who died before the unveiling. The memorial now graces the Market Place. *Postcard.*

131. When General William Booth, founder of the Salvation Army, embarked on a five-week motor campaign in 1909, his itinerary included Ossett. After passing through Chickenley Heath, the short motorcade proceeded down Church Street before arriving at the Town Hall. The General (rear seat, off-side) is pictured emerging into Dale Street on 6 August. *Postcard.*

132. The Ossett section of the West Riding Constabulary was photographed on 29 April 1912. At the Police Station on Prospect Road/Town End, Inspector William Denny was in charge of twelve men, and a smart no-nonsense mostly-moustached bunch they look! Ossett police moved to their new headquarters on Bank Street in 1993. The old premises (including the cells) were converted to a youth centre, which opened in 1996 and was renamed Brick House. *Postcard.*

133. Ossett's motor fire engine was purchased in 1913 for £1,100. Made by Merryweather, it is featured outside the brigade headquarters on Illingworth Street a few years later. It was affectionately known as Queen Mary and carried a name board denoting this. Its first attendance was at a fire at Ellis Mills on 31 December 1913. *Postcard: H Westmoreland, photographer, Ossett.*

134. The home of the Fawcett family and their business premises (near the railway bridge on The Green) are shown at left and right. The plumbing and glazing business was begun by Joseph Arthur Fawcett in 1895. He died in 1945 and son Henry Roland Fawcett took over. Also visible, behind the telephone box, is the cabin of Fred Wilby, tobacconist (note the baccy adverts). Houses have been built on the site of these buildings. *Photograph: courtesy Mr & Mrs David Hirst, St Andrews, Fife.*

135. Henry Roland Fawcett appears on this photograph (second right in the group) of a lorry decorated for a carnival. He served in the army during the 1914-18 War, was a teetotaller, and became a keen social worker. He was a member of various organisations, including the Dewsbury branch of the Federation of Master Plumbers and the Ossett Chamber of Trade. For many years in the 1930s, he was active in the Ossett Hospital & Convalescent Association carnivals. He was a member of Ossett Liberal Club and supported the Congregational Chapel on The Green. *Photograph: courtesy Mr & Mrs D Hirst, St Andrews.*

136. Henry Roland Fawcett, shown on the back row, right, was a member of the old part-time Ossett Fire Brigade and received a gold watch for his service when he retired, Here, he is seen attending the wedding of another volunteer fireman. *Photograph: courtesy Mr & Mrs D Hirst, St Andrews.*